Nature's Olympics

For Bekah Jorgensen —
I hope that you
enjoy my poems about
the natural world.
Best wishes!
      Janet Ruth Heller
      april 19, '22
      Portage MI

Nature's Olympics

Poems

by Janet Ruth Heller

RESOURCE *Publications* · Eugene, Oregon

NATURE'S OLYMPICS
Poems

Resource Publications
An Imprint of Wipf and Stock Publishers
199 W. 8th Ave., Suite 3
Eugene, OR 97401

www.wipfandstock.com

PAPERBACK ISBN: 978-1-6667-3073-9
HARDCOVER ISBN: 978-1-6667-2259-8
EBOOK ISBN: 978-1-6667-2261-1

Cover art by Lori McElrath Eslick originally appeared on the cover of *Cricket* in 2018; Cricket Magazine Group and Lori McElrath Eslick have granted first reprint rights.

Dedication

I would like to thank my family and friends for their encouragement while I worked on *Nature's Olympics*.
I am especially grateful to the members of my writers' group for their helpful comments: Molly Lynde-Recchia, Miriam Bat-Ami, Theresa Coty O'Neil, Hedy Habra, Andrea England, Danica Davidson, Linda Miles Coppens, and Jo Wiley. I also want to honor three people who did not live to see this book completed, my parents Joan Heller and Bill Heller and my teacher Barbara Gensler.

Nature's Olympics

SUMMER

AUTUMN

WINTER

SPRING

Acknowledgments

Previous versions of the following poems have appeared in magazines, journals, books, and anthologies.

"April Concert." *The Writer* 92, no. 11 (November 1979): 24; copyrighted 1979, Madover Media, LLC; rpt. in *Bird Verse Portfolios*, series 1, no. 2 (1985): n. p.; rpt. in Janet Ruth Heller. *Folk Concert: Changing Times.* Cochran, GA: Anaphora Literary, 2012. 84.

"Autumn Leaves." *Sugar Mule*, no. 41. Special Issue on Women Writing Nature (August 2012): 211. http://www.sugarmule.com/41.htm; rpt. in *Folk Concert: Changing Times.* 49.

"Backyard Mystery." *Traffic Stop* (chapbook). Georgetown, KY: Finishing Line, 2011. 20; rpt. in *Folk Concert: Changing Times.* 66.

"Backyard Visitors." *Seeding the Snow* 5, no. 2 (Fall/Winter 2011): 16.

"Bird Bingo." In *They Gave Us Life: Celebrating Mothers and Fathers in Haiku*, edited by Robert Epstein, 100. West Union, WV: Middle Island, 2017.

"Camping Near Cumberland Falls, Kentucky." *Folk Concert: Changing Times.* 61¬62.

"Canadian Encounter." *Folk Concert: Changing Times.* 63.

"Canoe Trip in Northern Wisconsin, 1962." *Folk Concert: Changing Times.* 21.

"Cherry Trees in Autumn" (in "Autumn Haiku"). In *Recipes for Readers from Michigan Authors and Illustrators*, 47. Grand Rapids: Michigan Reading Association, 2009; rpt. in *Folk Concert: Changing Times.* 75.

"Clarity." In *Women's Encounters with the Mental Health Establishment: Escaping the Yellow Wallpaper*, edited by Elayne Clift, 204. Binghampton, NY: Haworth, 2002; rpt. in *Folk Concert: Changing Times.* 54.

"Clover" (in "Spring Haiku"). *Ginyu*, no. 47 (July 25, 2010): 79; rpt. in *Folk Concert: Changing Times.* 74.

"Dad's Yahrzeit" (in "Summer Haiku"). *The Heron's Nest* 13, no. 2 (June 2011): 54; rpt. in *They Gave Us Life: Celebrating Mothers and Fathers in Haiku*, edited by Robert Epstein, 99. West Union, WV: Middle Island, 2017.

"Desert Chase." *Folk Concert: Changing Times*. 50.

"On Eating Raspberries from Our Garden in January." *Encore*, January 2014, 38.

"Elegy for a 'Possum." *Knot Magazine* (Fall/Winter, 2020). https://www.knotliteraturemagazine.com/janet-ruth-heller.

"Finches in April" (in "Spring Haiku"). *Seeding the Snow* 6, no. 1 (Spring/Summer 2012): 8; rpt. in *Folk Concert: Changing Times*. 74.

"Flamboyance." *Persimmon Tree* (Winter 2017). http://www.persimmontree.org/v2/winter-2017/poems-from-the-central-states/

"Fractals." *The CEA Critic* 76, no. 1 (March 2014): 132.

"Frogs in May" (in "Spring Haiku"). *Sugar Mule*, no. 41. Special Issue on Women Writing Nature (August 2012): 211. http://www.sugarmule.com/41.htm

"Haiku for Nancy" (in "Spring Haiku"). *The Poet* 15 (1977): 88.

"Haven." *Folk Concert: Changing Times*. 48.

"Ice Storm" (in "Winter Haiku"). *Folk Concert: Changing Times*. 73.

"Indian Summer." *The Pegasus Review* (September/October 1999): 5; rpt. in *Folk Concert: Changing Times*. 67.

"Inheritance (For Oma)." *Old Northwest Review* (Fall 2015): 113¬114.

"January Blizzard." *Poetry Leaves: Adult Contemporary Anthology*, edited by Emily Kazmierczak, 75. Waterford, MI: Waterford Township Public Library, 2020.

"January Thaw" (in "Winter Tanka Suite"). *A Collection of Poems by the Virginia, Rhode Island, and Nevada Society of Poets*, 121. Riverview, FL: The National Society of Published Poets, 1976.

"June Heat." *Capper's Weekly* 105, no.13 (June 22, 1983): 15.

"Legend" (in "Winter Haiku"). *Organic Gardening* 32, no.1 (January 1985): 138; rpt. in *Folk Concert: Changing Times.* 73.

"The Long Winter of 2014." *Encore*, March 2017, 43.

"Losing My Father." In *Traffic Stop.* 6; rpt. in Folk Concert: *Changing Times.* 69.

"Maples in November" (in "Autumn Haiku"). *Green's Magazine* 7, no. 1 (Autumn 1978): 8.

"Metamorphosis" (in "Spring Haiku"). *Bird Verse Portfolios*, series 1, no. 2 (1985): n. p.

"Moonstruck." *The Spoon River Quarterly* 7, no. 4 (Fall 1982): 54; rpt. in *Folk Concert: Changing Times.* 83.

"Nature's Olympics." *Encore*, January 2009, 43; rpt. in *Traffic Stop.* 18; rpt. in *Folk Concert: Changing Times.* 76.

"Nature Walk at Shenandoah National Park, August, 2010." *Knot Magazine* (Fall/Winter, 2020). https://www.knotliteraturemagazine.com/janet-ruth-heller.

"Once Raw and Red" (in "Spring Haiku"). *Paper Wasp* 16, no. 4 (Spring 2010): 1.

"Only June" (in "Summer Haiku"). *bottle rockets*, no. 44 (February 2021): 23.

"Pheasants Pace" (in "Winter Haiku"). *Berry Blue Haiku*, no. 3 (December 2010): 10.

"Picking Raspberries." *Wisconsin People & Ideas* (Fall 2010): 6; rpt. in *Encore*, Summer 2011, 35; rpt. in *Traffic Stop.* 21; rpt. in *Folk Concert: Changing Times.* 71¬72.

"Pink Gladioli" (in "Summer Haiku"). *Frogpond* 33, no. 3 (Fall 2010): 27; rpt. in *Folk Concert: Changing Times.* 73.

"Primavera." *Primavera* 2 (1976): 45.

"Rift" (in "Summer Haiku"). *Frogpond* 43, no. 3 (Fall 2020): 34.

"In the Salon" (in "Winter Haiku"). *The Frameless Sky* 14 (June 25, 2021).

"Skinny-Dipping, July, 1960." *Traffic Stop.* 3; rpt. in *Folk Concert: Changing Times.* 20.

"Snow Poem." *Modern Maturity*, December 1981/January 1982, 8; rpt. in *Traffic Stop.* 19; rpt. in *Folk Concert: Changing Times.* 82.

"Sparrows in November" (in "Autumn Tanka"). *Bird Verse Portfolios.* 1985. n. p.

"Spring, 2013." *Thirty Days: The Best of the Tupelo Press* 30/30 *Project's First Year*, edited by Marie Gauthier, 73. North Adams, MA: Tupelo, 2015.

"Spring in Chicago." *The Poet* 15 (1977): 71.; rpt. in *Folk Concert: Changing Times.* 41.

"A Thaw" (in "Spring Haiku"). *The Pegasus Review* (November/December 1999): 4; rpt. in *Folk Concert: Changing Times.* 74.

"Thoughts of You in Autumn" (in "Autumn Haiku"). *Canticum Novum* 1 (1973): 47.

"Transformation" (in "Spring Haiku"). *Light Year '85*, edited by Robert Wallace, 76. Cleveland: Bits, 1984.

"Tulips in July" (in "Summer Haiku"). *Organic Gardening* 32, no. 7 (July 1985): 110.

"Unveiling." *Poem*, no.123 (August, 2020): 7.

"Waves." *Poetry of the Year*, edited by Barbara Fischer, 19. North Babylon, NY: J. Mark, 1977.

"Wild Turkeys in Mississippi, May 16, 1863." *Crucible* 48 (Fall 2014): 59.

"Winter Concert" (in "Winter Haiku"). *Sugar Mule*, no. 41. Special Issue on Women Writing Nature (August 2012): 211. http://www.sugarmule. com/41.htm; rpt. in *Bear Creek Haiku*, no. 165 (August 2020): 29.

"Your Smile Sags" (in "Autumn Haiku"). *Mayfly*, no. 50 (Winter 2011): 13.

SUMMER

Nature's Olympics

Swimmers churn Atlanta pools,
runners streak down dusty tracks,
and gymnasts tumble and fly through the air.
While the Olympic torch burns overhead,
thousands cheer the athletes.

Here in Michigan, loons paddle near Isle Royale
and laugh like banshees
before they dive and disappear
in the evening mist.
Chipmunks dash across our yard
to capture seeds, stuffing their cheeks,
then scamper toward their burrows.
Goldfinches balance on sunflowers,
chickadees dart from food to swaying trees,
and hummingbirds fly backwards,
landing on tithonia like acrobats.

Picking Raspberries: Learning Perspective

1

The black raspberries are ripe
and the golden berries have just turned
from green to orange.

I begin on the east side
of the canes and slowly
work my way west,
picking first the dark purple berries
at eye level and then the ones hiding,
lower and lower, nearly touching the ground.

2

Berry picking is a lesson in perspective:
I would miss most of the fruit
if I refused to lower my eyes,
then stoop and bend.

I push aside leaves and canes
to find the round and juicy globes,
gently pulling the berries
until they fall into my palm.

3

I met three-year-old Braylon at a wedding.
While we waited to eat,
we played peek-a-boo and laughed.
We rang tiny bells
to urge the bride and groom to kiss.
Later, we danced to the DJ's music,
sashaying, jumping, and whirling.

Had I not bent down
to hold Braylon's small hands,
I would not have seen the party
from his point of view.

Haven

Weighed down by cares,
I walk along the lake path,
reach a garden
ablaze with red bee balm,
golden torch lilies,
and ten hummingbirds
playing tag—
a slice of Eden.

Skinny-Dipping, July, 1960

Ten sixth-grade girls camp overnight
on the shores of Lake Pokegama
with two counsellors.
After an open-fire cookout and cleanup,
we decide to take a twilight swim
in the dark waters.
Miles from civilization,
we strip naked
and, whispering,
enter the still lake.

I've never swum without clothes before
and welcome the sensation
of cool water on my arms and legs and breasts
and flowing like lava
between my thighs.

Canoe Trip in Northern Wisconsin, 1962

We carry our canoes and backpacks
down the thin strip of land separating the Chippewa River
and Lake Namekagon.
The portage completed,
we eight teenaged girls and one counsellor
re-embark as raindrops begin to fall.

Manitowish campers consider ourselves braver
than Girl Scouts, and we're proud of our canoeing,
having practiced sweeps, pull-tos, rudders, and J-strokes
on an obstacle course back on Boulder Lake.
We've also studied campcraft scientifically,
learning the proper knots for securing tents
and the best ways to build a fire.

So no storm can faze us.
The wind whips across the lake,
shoving waves toward our boats.
We move at a right angle to the troughs.
I'm in the bow, paddling hard
as Tina yells, "Stroke!"
The rain pelts our heads and shoulders,
but we grin and pull up our ponchos' hoods,
looking like monks in the wilderness.

Sandy, our counsellor, leads us in a chorus
of "The Life of a Voyageur."
Judy and I sing harmony.
Lightning saws a jagged edge
across the steel-gray sky.

Timid people would stick close to shore,
but we tough women cut straight across the lake
to find the outlet on Sandy's map.
When thunder booms like cosmic cannons,
we stop singing. We need the breath
for stretching our arms and torsos,
for plowing paddles through the deep water.

Drenched, we reach the outlet
and the more sheltered Flambeau River.
We chat happily, searching for our campsite.
Once there, Ellen and Sue pitch our tents,
I start a roaring fire,
and Gail mixes pizza from scratch
while the shadows gather.

To nine starving women,
the pizza and canned beans
are a gourmet feast.
We swap ghost stories in the dark woods,
then retire to wet tents and damp sleeping bags.
Loons and foxes call in the distance.

Rural Sculptures

Two lifelike sculptures of deer
bedeck a suburban lawn.
I slow my car to gaze.
Then three more deer bound onto the road,
two does and a buck,
his antlers like giant thorns.
I come to a dead stop.
All five deer freeze,
then trot across the street,
leaving me amazed.

Moonstruck

1

Moonrise:
a white sickle
mows the darkness.

2

The half-moon stretches
raw and red,
a wound at the horizon.

3

Ducks fly north,
their wings brushing
the face of the moon.

4

Clouds strum
the quarter-moon
like a harp.

Backyard Tragedy

A young chipmunk
scampers from our woods
through the bluegrass
to eat sunflower seeds.

He dashes across our deck,
sees us watching,
then takes cover.

Curious, he tries to drink
from our goldfish pond
but falls in,
struggles, desperate.

Mike rushes outside
with a shovel,
heaves the chipmunk
out of the water.

The tiny rodent
lies still in the sunlight.

Three crows arrive.
One lifts him
gingerly, then pecks.

The birds fight
over the warm corpse,
tear out chunks.

Family Reunion on a Rainy Day

Thunderstorms rattled
and rain fell all day,
so we could not swim,
canoe, ski, or sail
on Elkhart Lake.

Most adults played bridge and hearts,
but some of us dealt hands of crazy eights
and old maid to the children.
We served tea
as they do in England,
then sat on the couch and watched
our Packers thrash the Bears.

At seven, we took
the back roads
to our favorite restaurant
in New Holstein
where cooks feed hungry droves
with portions of steak
as big as footballs.

The skies cleared
and arching across the heavens
a double rainbow.

Pyrotechnics, July, 2013

1

I first built fires
at Camp Birch Trail,
starting with twigs,
slowly adding parts of branches
and then logs.
As the wood turned black,
it snapped and roared.
We campers sang folksongs.
Flames leapt up,
kindling the cold night air.

We contained the combustion
in hearths and bonfires,
but I loved the danger,
the risk of uncontrolled passion.

2

Lightning sets ablaze
parched trees in Arizona heat,
razes one hundred twenty-nine buildings,
forces six hundred people to leave their homes.
When the swirling winds shift
on the last day in June,
nineteen Granite Mountain Hotshots
on Yarnell Hill
perish fighting the firestorm.

We visit the memorial,
stunned into silence.

Elegy for a Feral Kitten

Born wild, you romped
in our garden,
pounced on crickets.
While tired mom watched
from our deck,
you and your siblings
pawed each other
and wrestled.

Your black body
and white feet whirled
as you chased rabbits,
birds, chipmunks.
Our yard became
your theater.

A heart attack
swept you offstage.

But you danced
through our summer
like Fred Astaire.

Summer Haiku

1

Pink gladioli
unfurl in sunshine.
I long for you.

2

Rift in clouds
pouring light—
waterfall.

3

Cat prowls after rain,
explores my new car,
stamps mud on panes.

4

Tulips swallow
red flowers
into swollen pods.

5

You scold me.
Cicadas click
from the juniper.

6

Dad's yahrzeit—
a white moth
clings to my window.

7

Fireflies float,
glow above shrubs,
snare mates.

8

Only June—
crabapple leaves
turn yellow.

9

Heat wave and hot flash,
Japanese fan—
relief.

10

Hummingbirds
on the trumpet vine
mute blossoms.

Unveiling

Today in Phoenix,
we unveil the modest headstone
that declares you our beloved father,
husband, and grandfather.
As we chant the Kaddish,
ducks and swans patrol
the pond near your grave.

I remember the times
you took Will and me to lagoons
in Milwaukee. We brought breadcrumbs
to feed the wildlife.
The heated lagoon on Lake Drive
attracted the big birds
even in winter,
and we watched distant ships
plying Lake Michigan.

On weekends, we hiked in Estabrook Park
and searched along the river
for trilobite fossils.
We visited the pond
to watch mallard ducks and white swans
glide by and hustle
to gulp down our bread.
Will often got too close
and fell in the water.
Then we had to go home
to get him dry clothes.

While we place pebbles on your grave,
the graceful swans
carry their cygnets
on their backs
and teach them to dive.

Comfort

In despair, I leave the retreat,
wounded by my friend's anger
and my enemy's attacks.
Maples reach out to me.
I ramble down a path.
Then three fawns and a doe
leap over a fence,
cross the dirt road,
nibble birch and sassafras.
The fawns play tag,
chasing one another in circles.
When they rest,
the doe nuzzles her brood.

Nature Walk at Shenandoah National Park, August, 2010 (For Patricia Clark and Miriam Pederson)

Alert for wildlife,
we emerge from our cabin,
take paths across forests and meadows.

We find a doe and her fawn
under a tall tree,
nibbling green Milam apples.

A crowd gathers.
We see movement among the leaves,
look for squirrels. No—

a black bear sits on a branch,
yanking and gobbling fruit,
dropping some for the deer.

Training the Teenaged Grackle

Red mouth open wide,
a young grackle trails his parent,
screeching like a rusty hinge.
The mother pokes the ground,
beak searching for worms or grubs.
Every few minutes,
she crams a snack
into the child's mouth,
then glares at the fledgling
as if planning a retort:
"Fend for yourself.
It's time you got a job."

Inheritance (For Oma)

A Japanese doll sat on your piano.
She looked startled to see me touch the keys.
You taught me how to play two songs
as the doll kept time.

Carrying my tiny parasol,
I helped you tend the garden.
We reveled in roses, tulips, and phlox.
Marigolds discouraged the bees.

I came with you to your art class.
We sketched a house and a crowded beach.
But your favorite theme was flowers:
still lifes covered your basement.

Now I write poetry in the town where you were born.
Green plants dangle across my apartment.
Your painting with three white blossoms
hangs over my bed.

Losing My Father

I lost my father in August.
But how can one misplace
a six-foot-one inventor,
a successful businessman?
When I was a child,
I had to take four steps
for one of his when we walked together.

A few days after Dad died,
I saw three deer behind our home.
The adult deer was very tall
and steered the fawns toward cover.
I wondered whether Dad's spirit
had entered the tall parent.

We used to call him Daddy-Longlegs.
Now I can't kill these insects
when they invade my home.

Driving down Crosstown Parkway,
I saw a blue heron in the pond.
Skinny and towering over the ducks and geese,
he resembled my father.

Where are you now, Dad?
I lift up my eyes and see
the stars and constellations
you showed me when I was young.
Are you resting on the Big Dipper?

I miss you.
Hover beside me as I walk,
and when I lose my way,
help me find the North Star.

AUTUMN

Flamboyance (For Oma)

You took me to the fancy Schroeder Hotel
for lunch, though I was only five.
My hamburger and Coke probably cost a fortune.
But I was your oldest grandchild.

Under the chandeliers,
Your necklace and bracelet glittered.
You showed me your paintings of goldfinches and roses
from the morning's art class.
"I wish I could draw like that."
"I'll show you how to sketch.
"I always wanted a daughter," you declared.

Then you slid my straw's wrapper down,
squeezing the paper
until it turned into a snake.
We spooned water drops onto the serpent
to make it slither.
Knowing my mother would not approve
this trick, I giggled with delight.

As we ate, we watched tall women
mount a platform in the center of the restaurant
to display the latest autumn fashions.
They glided through the crowd like queens.

When the last model descended from the platform,
I ran up the steps and twirled
in my red and gold pinafore,
dancing like the maple leaves outside,
on fire with turbulent desire.

Autumn Haiku

1

After a rainstorm,
I perch in the cherry tree,
float in a gold sea.

2

Maple leaves swirl.
Bright orange pumpkins
bounce in the combine.

3

From the sassafras,
finches cross-examine me,
lawyers in red hoods.

4

Thick clouds diffract
October sunset—
pink ribbons.

5

Across the pavement,
gingko leaves—
golden fans.

6

Your smile sags—
a jack-o-lantern
left in the rain.

7

Thoughts of you
cling to me—
brown oak leaves.

8

Maples stand naked,
spines
of my summer dreams.

9

No leaves
on the dead ash tree
but threescore starlings.

10

Cherry branches
dance in the wind and dangle
black bead necklaces.

Time Travel, October, 2017

I hike in late October
wearing a sleeveless shirt.
Global warming threatens the earth,
but I love basking in the sun's rays.

This autumn, time travels in reverse,
refusing to sail toward winter.
Can adults unravel our days,
return to childhood?

When I was eight,
teachers showed a film about industry.
We students begged them to rewind,
leaving the projector in gear.

We laughed as people ran backwards,
cars reversed their journeys,
and chopped down trees
regained their upright posture.

Climate change slows the fall of leaves,
revives old memories.

Buck in November

A buck
with tiny antlers
hobbles
around our yard,
his right front leg
curled, never touching
the ground.

How will he survive
the coming storms?

Autumn Leaves

Leaves like gold coins
fall from ornamental pear trees
while tulip poplars shed
multi-hued flowers.
Sweetgums drop
red and yellow stars.

But oak trees hoard
their dry brown leaves
that rattle in the wind
like my obsessions.

Guest

When maple leaves
turned red and yellow,
an albino house finch
graced our yard,
ate sunflower seeds
with brown and rose friends,
splashed in our birdbath.

The white finch returned
on many afternoons,
shone like a star,
but left before the snow.

Season of Gold

This October,
most shrubs and trees
shimmer with gold:
shagbark hickory,
sugar maple, silver maple,
tulip poplar, crab apple,
cottonwood, black locust,
aspen, birch, gingko,
butternut, and sycamore.

Only Japanese maple,
sumac, scarlet oak,
and burning bush
flaunt red leaves.

Will a new Golden Age
arise on earth?
I hold my breath,
hoping for a miracle.

AUTUMN TANKA

Sparrows in November

Sparrows bathe in a puddle.
One beats his wings,
splashes friends.
Defying the icy wind,
they carouse like drunks.

Black Cherries

After summer rain,
black cherries swell
to the size of chickpeas.
When autumn storms hit,
cherries pelt the roof like hail.

Wild Turkey

Wild turkey struts
across our yard,
eats sunflower seeds and corn,
then flies to our deck,
her new throne.

Deer

If I were not human,
I would like to be a deer,
emerging from the forest
on slender legs
without warning,
romping in meadows,
jumping fences,
invading gardens,
nibbling apples, leaves,
corn, tulips, and roses,
nudging friends,
brandishing antlers,
luminous in the night.

Backyard Visitors

1

The fox squirrels
have no trusts,
no stocks or bonds,
no real estate.
But they bury acorns
that grow into oak trees,
providing nuts
for grandchildren.

2

A huge 'possum
with sad eyes
ambles across our yard
one afternoon
and disappears
into the woods.

3

A buck and a doe
explore our shrubs.
He parades full antlers
while she decapitates
our last rose.

4

The red squirrel races
from our feeder with corn
to a spruce.

When fox squirrels
approach the grain,
he chases them away,
though they're three times
the size of this brave
little champion.

Fall Color, October, 2016

Michigan has warm days,
cool nights, and rain,
the formula for fall color.
Redbuds display yellow hearts,
and maples turn scarlet.
Midas touches black locusts
and shagbark hickories,
transforming their compound leaves
into gold.
Burning bushes blaze
against the blue sky.
Yellow dominates
half of the sassafras,
while red tinges the rest.
Roses, hibiscus, morning glories,
candy tufts, hydrangea, phlox,
and a rainbow of mums
revel in blooms.

Indian Summer

When it's seventy degrees in October,
I see everything with the eyes of a child.

The bushes wave arms red as candy
against the sky, blue as a popsicle.
Elm leaves fly past like golden birds
escaping from a fairytale.

Catalpa pods
sway in the breeze;
silent chimes,
enchanted by a local witch.

Just fallen ginkgo leaves
pile up like doubloons
hoarded by a pirate.

Fat squirrels hop after chestnuts,
then curl up in burrows
to dream of spring.

At night the moon plays
peek-a-boo
behind the tall buildings.

WINTER

On Eating Raspberries from Our Garden in January

The sweet, sharp taste of raspberries
explodes in my mouth,
hurling memories of summer heat,
summer storms, summer journeys.

I remember rinsing the tiny beehives
and freezing them separately like jewels,
then putting the hardened fruit
into bags like children's marbles.

Now snow falls and icy winds bellow
from the west and from the north.
But inside of me is a warm glow
and the taste of summer on my tongue.

Backyard Mystery

Some animal raids our yard at night,
ripping divots in the lawn
like a lousy golfer.

We suspect the fat local groundhog,
but he waddles by day
and doesn't eat grass, worms, or grubs.

Then we suspect the raccoon,
but she eludes us,
except for one visit to our deck.

I stay up late after a snowfall,
peer out the back window.
A full moon spotlights
the culprit: a dark and handsome skunk.

Elegy for a 'Possum

For weeks, we had found
tiny paw prints
coming up our snow-covered sidewalk,
climbing the porch step,
proceeding west
around our house,
and crossing the backyard.
We thought the paws
belonged to a kitten.
But the kind people on our block
would never abandon
such a young pet.

One February night
at ten o'clock, we met
the creature: a small 'possum
slowly walking toward us.
His eyes drooped
as if he were sad,
and his white face
glowed starkly in the porch light.

He slowly grew
to adult size and strength.
We heard his grunts
like barks of a dog with a cold.
Sometimes we encountered him
when carrying our scraps
to the compost bin
or when we returned
from a late walk
to find the 'possum
in our garden.

Every summer, the creature
took a shortcut
across our front lawn,
wearing a diagonal path
from the driveway to the porch.
Every winter, we traced
his tracks in the snowfall,
noting his short legs
and his dragging tail.

This spring, we think he fell ill
or fought with a cat
or got hit by a car.
Our neighbors found his body
wedged under their ramp.
We buried him in our woods
with full honors.

January Blizzard

Twenty-one inches of snow
swaddle Chicago.

Drifts swirl into giant egg whites
whipped stiff by the wind.

The streets fall silent:
neither humans nor cars can move.

One stalled automobile
displays a hand-made sign:
Rest in Peace.

Snow Poem

Languid flakes cover familiar images,
bringing me metaphors
in crystalline form.

Trees resemble giant white flowers.
Among their branches, light
plays hide and seek.

Fog bites off the heads
of distant buildings
like a hungry dragon.

Snow arches over
windows and doors, sketching
bushy eyebrows and moustaches.

Cars huddle like moles,
blinded by the storm.
Bicycles become cubist statues.

Like a witch, I hoard
all the images
for my winter brew.

Winter Haiku

1

Willows' brown hair
turns gray in the hoarfrost.
Wind combs it back.

2

Rabbit tracks flitter
on powder-light snowfall—
butterfly wings.

3

Across the prairie,
corn stubs bend, scrawl
Sanskrit in furrows.

4

Mike starts a fight,
tells me I'm stupid.
Deer piss on snow.

5

Vivian's funeral—
hoarfrost coats the maples
sparkling in the sun.

6

Snow falls in Tucson,
quieting the wrens.
Cacti sport scarves, caps.

7

Frozen trees wait.
Before the curtain,
dancers pose.

8

Hopping across snow,
juncos disappear
in Mike's bootprint.

9

In the salon, gold hair
drifts from grandmothers.
Snow falls at sunset.

10

Gray morning at six:
we shiver with the bare tree.
Red cardinal sings!

11

Pheasants pace
on white drifts—
Great-Grandma crochets.

12

Twelve inches of snow
overwhelm the crocuses,
seal purple mouths shut.

Snowstorm

The wind whips against me
as I stumble home

in the darkness,
dazed and blinded by snow.

I must learn to walk again,
knees bent, leaning forward.

I whisper thanks for the pioneers
who made the tracks ahead.

Now I know why farmers perish in storms,
crossing from their field to the barn.

The Long Winter of 2014

Winter attacked us like a mugger,
battering us with frigid winds, hail,
whiteouts that closed roads
and shattered the power grid.

Snow piled fifteen feet high
obliterated mailboxes and froze solid,
blocking letters from friends,
jailing us in our homes.

The cold and storms
held us hostage for three months.
Even deer hunkered down,
unable to walk through high drifts.

Then we had a brief thaw
followed by rain
that turned into a blizzard
and axed tree limbs.

Now in late March, winter slowly frees us
from bondage. Snow begins to melt,
but the compressed crystals
resemble harpoons.

Today, the crocus blooms,
displays lavender petals
that dare winter to strike again.

Inter-Species Communication (For M.C.)

Up north in Emmet County,
chipmunks bore a hole
in Mary's toolshed,
set up homestead,
and leave a stack
of earth, acorns, and hickory shells.

During spring cleaning
at her cabin, Mary
discovers the intrusion,
sweeps up the pile,
and hammers two boards
to cover the hole.

"This is my shed,"
she tells the rodents.
"My family has owned this property
for two generations.
I work hard all year
and come here for vacations."

The chipmunks scold her
from a fallen log ten feet away.
"You squatter!" they shout.
"You spent all winter
in your fancy warm condo
back in Kalamazoo

while we froze here,
tried to sleep through storms,
and repaired
our underground lair.
Go home,
and leave our den alone!"

WINTER TANKA SUITE

Sleet

Sleet falls,
coating tree branches
with ice half an inch thick;
boughs bend, snap,
explode.

Moonlight

The full moon highlights
tree shadows against new snow,
surreal art. Afraid to expose
dark bodies, rabbits, deer,
and 'possums hide.

January Thaw

Feathery clouds
and plumes from airplanes
transform the sky
into an inverted rink
crisscrossed by skate blades.

Driving down Route 23 after Work in a Blizzard

Snow blazes in my headlights,
rushing toward me
with images of my students,
fragmented like fireworks,
dazzling my tired eyes.

Jana Pleads with the Moon

I whisper to the full moon,
"You are beautiful."
She stares in silence.

I cry to the full moon,
"I yearn to touch you!"
She covers herself with a cloud.

I scream to the full moon,
"I love you!"
She sets in a blaze of red.

Blood Moon

After days of snowstorms,
we get a clear, cold night
for this lunar eclipse.
Like a hungry child,
the earth bites
large moon chunks
until the white orb
turns blood red.

Native Americans call this
the howling Wolf Moon,
but scientists name it
a Super Blood Moon.
Now the satellite comes
so close to our blue planet,
a girl running
toward her parent.

Mom died two years ago.
I miss her, wish I could tell
her about the total eclipse,
have one more embrace.
Grief rends my heart
like a ravening wolf,
and a red mist
clouds my sight.

Fractals

Fronds of ferns
replicate the whole plant,
and oak trees branch
into fractal twigs.

After rain, broccoli
florets sprout.
Jack Frost paints
fractals on windows.

Mountain ranges
iterate peaks,
and seacoasts swirl
into fractal curves.

Scalloped clouds
vaporize,
and lightning forks
into fractal strikes.

Blood vessels
divide fractally,
forming streams
and rivers.

Ice storms smash
trees to the ground,
snap branches like firecrackers,
but spring will birth new fractals.

SPRING

Bird-Watching

We watch the pheasant
strut across our yard
to eat corn and sunflower seeds.
He ascends a pile of dirt left by bulldozers,
then flaps his huge wings
and crows like a hoarse rooster.
Our lot is his territory.
His plumage shimmers
with red, gold, and green
like the double rainbow overhead.

2

The pheasant watches us eat dinner
and wonders why we change our feathers every day
and wonders why we don't eat seeds
and wonders why we make such strange noises
and wonders why we need wheels to travel
and wonders where we go from nine to five
and wonders why we dig up his beloved mounds
and wonders why we sleep so late
when he awakens before the dawn
and wonders why we stare at him
so intently.

Release

After a winter so harsh
that I wrapped myself
in sweaters and quilts,
and my finger tips
turned as white as a corpse,

spring arrives like a bride,
scattering green shoots in the loam
and buds on magnolia,
opening the crocus and daffodil.

I take my first walk
without a scarf,
without a coat.

Spring in Chicago

Skyscrapers mute
the golden trumpet of sunlight.

We muffle greetings,
fear retaliation.

The March quickening
in this oasis of culture
yields a harvest
of partial fruit.

Suicide in March, 1997 (For the Heaven's Gate Cult)

Crocuses open their mouths wide
to swallow sunlight
after a fierce Michigan winter.
Far away in San Diego,
thirty-nine followers
of Heaven's Gate Cult
open their mouths
to swallow vodka and phenobarbital,
then wrap their heads in plastic bags.
Devotees believe a spaceship
will transport them to salvation.
Comet Hale-Bopp blazes
across the night sky.

Spring, 2013

Cold winds blew
in April, May, and June,
freezing the cherry blossoms
but sparing the apples and rhubarb.

In July, rain fell often,
fattening the black raspberries
and thrusting the daylilies
five feet above the ground.

Today, the rose of Sharon
in our front yard
burst into bloom,
white petals with a blood-red heart.

Spring Haiku

1

Hoarfrost crumbles
and falls from branches—
broken chains.

2

Snow retreats,
exposing daffodils.
My anger abates.

3

We fill the feeder
with corn, but deer
eat our tulips.

4

After sunset, frogs
sing high-pitched notes—
counter-tenor ghosts.

5

Clover defies drought
to spread across our yard.
My love for you grows.

6

Dandelions flutter,
fly away as we approach.
No—golden warblers!

7

Mike plays his fiddle.
Chipmunks and cardinals
form a quartet.

8

Under the hairdryer,
your slim body dangles—
a mushroom stem.

9

Red peony sprouts—
soldiers brandish
bayonets.

10

Thrushes warble.
When I caress you,
sinews trill.

11

Once raw and red,
my scar heals.
The new moon rises.

12

Mike leaves his Honda
in the spring rain. It will grow
into a Buick.

Eden

This spring I tried to force
a hyacinth and your love
to grow in my parlor.
Nothing flowered.

Next spring I'll try tulips.

Growing Up on the Other Side of Lake Michigan, an Ode (For Judith Minty)

My father proposed to my mother
on a bluff above Lake Michigan.

I was born a mile west of the lake
as the sun rose over Milwaukee.

When I was a toddler,
we moved north to Green Bay.
I remember the empty lot on our block
where I played with friends
and chased my baby brother
through the purple clover and Queen Anne's lace.
I visited a neighbor
who grew corn and vegetables.
During the cold winters,
snow fell on the lake.

We returned to Milwaukee when I was five.
Will and I stayed with Oma, our grandmother,
while Mom and Dad unpacked boxes
and cleaned our new house
in Whitefish Bay.

At school, if someone delayed
the line for the drinking fountain,
classmates would shout,
"Don't drink the whole lake!"

Mom drove us kids to Atwater Beach to swim.
I felt like an ice cube in the cold waves.
Dad took us to see ducks and swans
in the lagoon on Lake Drive.
Kenny, our babysitter, claimed
that he painted the lake,
using different colors every day.

When I was nine,
we moved to Shorewood.
Now there were four kids,
and we needed more space.
We had a huge yard with spruce trees.
Every winter Dad made a rink,
enabling us to skate.
We built snow mountains
with our playmates.

Dad took us for walks in Lake Park
and told us stories about his Army days
in France and Germany
living in a tent, keeping guard at night,
and making maps for General Patton.
Dad taught us how to test a bridge
so troops could safely reach
the other side.
We held on tightly
to the guardrails while our feet
probed the span's planks.

When I was old enough to shop alone,
I used Lake Michigan to navigate:
It was always due east.
Gimbel's and Chapman's were closer to the lake
than the Boston Store.

My friend Sue lived on Lake Michigan.
She invited every kid in our class
to her birthday party in May.
We floated on her tire swing,
climbed to her garage roof,
feasted on barbecued hamburgers
and homemade chocolate cake.
At the climax of every party,
the boys threw all the girls
into the cold lake.

During my college years,
I took my boyfriend Tzvi to Lake Drive
for a romantic walk along the shore.
When Fred broke up with me,
I watched rain pour into the lake.

I went south to Chicago
to work on my doctorate.
Thieves slugged me
and stole my purse,
but I kept studying for exams.
I wrote a book of poetry
and a dissertation
tracing the history
of bias against performed tragedy.
From my Hyde Park apartment,
I could see a tiny piece of the lake.

I taught creative writing
on Michigan Avenue.
The tenth-floor classroom
had picture windows
and a terrific lake view.

My wordsmith friends and I
assembled in Ann's solarium
near Hyde Park Drive.
We could trace the coast
all the way to Indiana.
I joked that historians would label us
the Lake Michigan Poets.

I met Mike on Chanukah at Temple Sinai,
the radical Reform synagogue
which friends called
"St. Sinai by the Sea."
I married Mike at Rodfei Tzedek,
a shul closer to the tradition
and overlooking Lake Michigan.

Seven years later,
we moved to Kalamazoo.
Looking west to see the waves
disorients me.
"Water's on the wrong side here," I complain.
A Michigan native,
Judith reprimands:
"Just watch the sunsets over the lake!"

Primavera

Jade-green grasses appear without warning
across the thawed earth's crust;

daffodils vie with newborn crocuses
for the precious rays of sunlight;

trees lace the sky
with their budding filaments;

the breeze secretly scatters
tiny packages of pollen;

cats, dogs, and other quadrupeds
prepare for an orgy of mating;

while I lie in bed,
swathed in handkerchiefs,
allergic to the spring.

April Concert

The red-breasted thrush
warbles a love song
to his pregnant lady
from the top of a sycamore.
She yodels back in antiphony
from her perch
on a nearby elm.

They sing so gaily
that a German shepherd
leans out the window to listen.

Bird Bingo

We used to play bird bingo
with Mom on rainy days,
matching pictures
of bright blue buntings,
saffron finches,
and orange orioles.

Fifty years later
on a sunny May afternoon,
birds spring from the bingo cards:
male and female indigo buntings
drink from our pond.

CAMPING NEAR CUMBERLAND FALLS, KENTUCKY

Hiking

Mike chooses the hardest trail in the park.
I pant along behind him
up and down rocky slopes.

I hear rustling among the bushes.
My scream dies away when I see a tiny lizard
fleeing from us two giants. Mike laughs.
"There are poisonous snakes,"
I remind him. He chuckles,
"The rattlesnakes and cottonmouths
are park employees!"

Then we hear water swirling loudly,
reach Eagle Falls.

Meals

As we grill steaks,
a red pileated woodpecker
drills for insects
in a tall Southern pine.
Hummingbirds hover over the shadbush,
bees wallow in mountain laurel,
and a young gray squirrel
attacks our garbage bag.

Wilderness Library

The rain drones on all afternoon,
confining us to the waterproof tent.
Perched on my sleeping bag,
I read Wilde's essays,
while bourgeois Mike studies *The Wall Street Journal*.
We could do a commercial for the A. L. A.

Insomnia

Still awake at midnight,
I listen for wolves and bears.
Something is clawing the tent,
turning this way and that,
ravenous for food.
Terrified, I burrow in my sleeping bag,
making similar noises, and realize
the "bear" is restless Mike.

Disorientation

All June, a doe bounds
into our yard at mid-day
and stays for an hour.
Have heavy rains
confused her nocturnal clock?

The doe devours violet leaves,
beheads hosta,
roses, lilies, and phlox.
Why is she so hungry?
Why does she tarry here?

Then one afternoon,
she gallops
across our lawn
and, trotting behind her,
a tiny fawn.

The Quiet before the Storm

Clouds block sunshine,
the wind subsides,
trees stand stock still,
the humidity rises,
and birds mute their calls.

Today my cousin reveals
that she has cancer.
She used to climb high
in blue spruce and play
drums and basketball.

I worry that a terrible storm
and wild winds will come,
uprooting trees,
ripping power lines,
and smashing homes.

But only light rain drops
from parting clouds.
Sunset paints the sky
pink and orange and purple.
No doom yet descends.

Canadian Encounter

Lost tourists, we stop near Kagawong.
An Indian in a broad-brimmed hat drives up
and begins to fish in the lake.
Mike asks him the way to Bridal Veil Falls.
The Indian points to a path through the woods:
"Follow the river," he says.

Like a water snake, the river twines among the rocks,
its rapids too treacherous for a canoe.
We trip on the stony trail,
pass white musk mallow
and orange jewelweed shaped like moccasins.

The falls are worth all our stumbling:
water drops like beadwork from the limestone cliff.
While Mike climbs to photograph the chute,
I search for more wildflowers
and find delicate purple bellflowers
enclosed by three Molson bottles.

When we return to the lake,
the Indian is catching a bass.
Mike starts the car.
I wave to the fisherman,
and he waves back.

Desert Chase

Breathless, I run toward you.
But the desert between us
stretches to the horizon.
Saguaros bend their arms
in gestures of despair.

You call from the distance.
I race toward your figure,
but it is a mirage.
The prickly pear scratches my legs.

We meet at an oasis,
drink from the brook.
You sneer at my torn clothes
and my dust-covered body.
The mockingbird screams.

Under a sky burning
like the scorpion's sting,
we part again.

Wild Turkeys in Mississippi, May 16, 1863

Wild turkeys scamper
through the woods and meadows
near Champion Hill.
They search for seeds
under the willow oaks
and the magnolias.

Today they find bags of corn
ripped open,
bowls of grits smashed,
tents toppled,
and strange forms
in the ravines.

Frightened, the turkeys flee
the groaning animals
dressed in blue and gray,
their bodies ripped and smashed.

Spring, 2020

During the pandemic,
April and May frosts
shrivel fruits and flowers
on lilacs, apple trees,
plums, cherries,
peaches, and magnolias.

But trillium, dame's rocket,
dandelions, redbuds,
violets, honeysuckle,
dogwood, and azalea
proliferate.

An uneasy spirit
disrupts and pervades
towns, woods, and prairies.
People groan, crowds wail,
wrens shriek,
and coyotes howl.

June Heat

The ninety-degree heat
makes everything lazy.

Ash leaves hardly move
when nudged by the breeze.

Windows across the street
yawn open.

Young children
squat languidly on doorsteps.

I lie down
to take my second nap.

Clarity

After I talk with you,
the heat wave lifts
and the air clears.

I can see every leaf
on the oaks and maples,
and, drifting from the cottonwood,
a million tiny parachutes.

Love-note in June

Dandelion spores
float
lighter than snow
this overcast June day.

Dreams of you
waft my heart away.

All my thoughts come to rest
with your head between my breasts.

All Love Is Equal*

Today, five judges in black robes
decree that marriage transcends
one man and one woman.
Now Adam can wed Steve
and Beth can marry Eve
because all love is equal.

Nature celebrates the verdict:
yellow roses blossom,
astilbe wave in the breeze,
and raspberries ripen.

Lovers everywhere rejoice:
fireflies glow,
frogs sing in the pond,
rabbits gambol,
turkeys strut,
and purple martins
maneuver like jets.

* On June 26, 2013, the U.S. Supreme Court issued a 5 to 4
  decision declaring Section 3 of the Defense of Marriage Act
  to be unconstitutional "as a deprivation of the liberty of the
  person protected by the Fifth Amendment" ("*United States
  v. Windsor*," in *Wikipedia*).

Janet Ruth Heller

Janet Ruth Heller is president of the Michigan College English Association and also served as a past president of the Society for the Study of Midwestern Literature. She has a Ph.D. in English Language and Literature from the University of Chicago and has taught literature, creative writing, linguistics, composition, and women's studies courses at eight colleges and universities.

Heller has published three other books of poetry: *Exodus* (WordTech Editions, 2014), *Folk Concert: Changing Times* (Anaphora Literary Press, 2012), and *Traffic Stop* (Finishing Line Press, 2011). She is a founding mother and former editor of *Primavera*, an award-winning literary magazine. The University of Missouri Press published her scholarly book, *Coleridge, Lamb, Hazlitt, and the Reader of Drama* (1990). Her essay "A Visit to Isle Royale" was aired over Michigan Public Radio (1999). Her creative nonfiction "Returning to Elkhart Lake, Wisconsin" appeared in *Midwestern Miscellany* (2008). Her play *The Cell Phone* won fourth place in a national contest and was performed at the Fenton Village Players One-Act Play Festival in Fenton, Michigan (2011). Her play *Pledging* was performed at Triton College in Illinois as part of the Tritonysia Play Festival in 2017.

Heller's fiction picture book about bullying, *How the Moon Regained Her Shape* (Arbordale, 2006; 6th edition 2018), has received many awards, including a Book Sense Pick (2006), a Children's Choices selection (2007), a Benjamin Franklin Award (2007), and a Gold Medal in the Moonbeam Children's Book Awards (2007). She has also published *The Passover Surprise* (Fictive Press, 2015, 2016), a middle-grade fiction chapter book for children. Her website is *https://www.janetruthheller.com*

CPSIA information can be obtained
at www.ICGtesting.com
Printed in the USA
LVHW080007281121
704581LV00005BA/20